Raptor World

Hawks

by Jenna Lee Gleisner

Bullfrog Books

Ideas for Parents and Teachers

Bullfrog Books let children practice reading informational text at the earliest reading levels. Repetition, familiar words, and photo labels support early readers.

Before Reading

- Discuss the cover photo. What does it tell them?
- Look at the picture glossary together. Read and discuss the words.

Read the Book

- "Walk" through the book and look at the photos. Let the child ask questions. Point out the photo labels.
- Read the book to the child, or have him or her read independently.

After Reading

- Prompt the child to think more. Ask: Red-tailed hawks are the most common hawks in North America. They can often be seen on the sides of roads, looking for prey. Have you seen a hawk?

Bullfrog Books are published by Jump!
5357 Penn Avenue South
Minneapolis, MN 55419
www.jumplibrary.com

Library of Congress Cataloging-in-Publication Data

Names: Gleisner, Jenna Lee, author.
Title: Hawks / by Jenna Lee Gleisner.
Description: Bullfrog books edition.
Minneapolis, MN : Jump!, Inc., [2020]
Series: Raptor World
Audience: Age 5-8. | Audience: K to Grade 3.
Includes index.
Identifiers: LCCN 2018040552 (print)
LCCN 2018041699 (ebook)
ISBN 9781641286312 (e-book)
ISBN 9781641286305 (hardcover : alk. paper)
ISBN 9781641288224 (pbk.)
Subjects: LCSH: Hawks—Juvenile literature.
Classification: LCC QL696.F32 (ebook)
LCC QL696.F32 G595 2020 (print)
DDC 598.9/44—dc23
LC record available at https://lccn.loc.gov/2018040552

Editor: Susanne Bushman
Designer: Jenna Casura

Photo Credits: Antagain/iStock, cover; Sergio Gutierrez Getino/Shutterstock, 1; SteveMcsweeny/iStock, 3; Georgia Evans/Shutterstock, 4, 23bl; GUIDO BISSATTINI/Shutterstock, 5, 23bm; Ian Duffield/Shutterstock, 6–7; Noppadon stocker/Shutterstock, 8–9, 23tm; Matt Jeppson/Shutterstock, 10, 23br; Stefonlinton/iStock, 11; Ronnie Howard/Shutterstock, 12; Tze-hsin Woo/Getty, 12–13; JosieN/iStock, 14; Mark Hamblin/Age Fotostock, 15; Ondrej Prosicky/Shutterstock, 16–17; Danita Delimont/Alamy, 18–19, 23tl; Don Mammoser/Shutterstock, 20–21; backlitcoyote/iStock, 22; Ad_hominem/Shutterstock, 23tr; GlobalP/iStock, 24.

Printed in the United States of America at Corporate Graphics in North Mankato, Minnesota.

Table of Contents

Good Hunters

A bird sits on a perch.

It is a hawk!

It looks for prey.

Like what?

Mice. Rabbits. Snakes.

tail

Many hawks live in North America.

The red-tailed hawk is the most common.

See its red tail?

Cool!

Hawks have great eyesight.

They can see colors we can't!

It sees a snake slither.

It takes off!

The hawk digs in.
With what?
Its talons.
They are sharp!

It carries it back to its nest. This one has a nest in a tree.

This hawk has a nest in the grass.

Rip!

The hawk tears each piece off.

Its beak helps.

chick

The mom feeds her chicks.

They do not have their red tails yet.

They grow up
and hunt, too.

Built to Hunt

wings
A hawk's wings are broad, rounded, and strong. The average wingspan is 4 feet (1.2 meters).

beak
The sharp beak is hooked. It helps the hawk tear its food before eating it.

talons
Sharp talons help hawks catch, carry, and hold onto prey.

Picture Glossary

chicks
Baby hawks.

eyesight
The ability to see.

North America
The continent made of the United States, Canada, Mexico, and Central America.

perch
A raised place where something sits.

prey
Animals that are hunted by other animals for food.

slither
To move along by sliding.

Index

To Learn More

Finding more information is as easy as 1, 2, 3.

1. Go to www.factsurfer.com
2. Enter "hawks" into the search box.
3. Click the "Surf" button to see a list of websites.